TI......s
Gu.....

Leadership

Shelly Newstead

The Big Buskers Guide to Leadership

ISBN 978-1-904792-17-8

Published by Common Threads Publications Ltd
Wessex House
Upper Market Street
Eastleigh
Hampshire SO50 9FD
T: 02380 629460
E: info@commonthreads.org.uk
W: www.commonthreads.org.uk

Other titles in The Buskers Guide series include:
The Buskers Guide to Playwork
The Buskers Guide to Behaviour
The Buskers Guide to Inclusion
The Buskers Guide to Playing Out
The Buskers Guide to Anti-Discriminatory Practice
The Buskers Guide to Risk
The Buskers Guide to Participation

The text of 'The Buskers Guide...' series can be made available in 14 point font - please contact the publishers by telephoning 02380 629460 or emailing info@commonthreads.org.uk

The Big Buskers Guide to Leadership

Contents

Introduction   **page 2**

Chapter 1   **Who, me?**   **page 3**

Chapter 2   **Mission - impossible?**   **page 17**

Chapter 3   **A mission shared ...**   **page 41**

Chapter 4   **The art of persuasion ...**   **page 51**

And finally...   **page 68**

Chapter 1
Who, me?

Hello – and welcome to another 'Buskers Guide'! Only as you've no doubt already noticed, this one's a bit different – well, more different than usual for a Buskers Guide, perhaps I should say! – as it has been written for a very specific group of people. So before we start proper, I just need to check that you're the right person reading the right book!

The first thing that is hopefully true about you is that you are working in some sort of childcare or playwork type of setting. As with all the 'Buskers', you could be in any type of setting within that huge field, be that a very small pre-school playgroup or a large national chain of after-school clubs, or indeed anything in-between – we don't discriminate with our 'Buskers Guides' readership!

But this is a 'Big Buskers', and more specifically, 'The Big Buskers Guide to Leadership'. So I am hoping that you are in some sort of role that involves you leading other people in your setting – or to put it another way, that your job role involves you being 'in charge' of other people in some way, shape or form! Your official title might be manager, supervisor, leader, head, deputy (manager/supervisor/leader…), room leader… take your pick, and I'm sure there's lots more variations on a theme out there! But from our point of view, any and all of those titles, and any like them, all have one thing in common – they all mean that you have professional responsibility for other people's work in your setting.

(By the way, it could also be the case I guess that you are reading this book because you are thinking of applying for a job which involves some sort of leadership role – in which case, good luck and there's an email address somewhere in this book, I'd be very interested to hear how you get on!)

So if we're all happy that you are indeed the right person reading the right book, we'll get the ball rolling…by going back to the start!

I said earlier that all of those job titles had something in common – that they all involved having a professional responsibility for other people's work. And in order to get to grips with 'leadership', we need to understand that as somebody in a leadership capacity, it is our job to influence other people – and more specifically, to influence other people's professional practice.

And it's important that we get this clear in our minds straight away, because being a leader/manager/supervisor etc in our field can often be confused with many other things. In some settings, the person in charge is also known as 'she (and it usually is 'she' in our case) who must be obeyed'. In other words, the ultimate authority, the boss, the person who is always right – particularly when she is wrong! In other settings, the person who has the dubious pleasure of being 'the leader' (and usually, but not always, unfortunately, the person on the slightly higher pay rate) is the person who gets to do all the paperwork – oh the joy and the job satisfaction! And in many settings, 'leadership' is seen as some sort of bizarre reward for being a really good practitioner – you're so good at it, we'll put you in charge! – and then everybody expects you not only to be able to do everything plus your new leadership role, but also to do it all better than everybody else put together!

Now it is true unfortunately that some of us just don't help ourselves when it comes to these rather dubious ideas of what 'leadership' is about...For example, lots of leaders I've met seem hell-bent on proving to the rest of their setting that they jolly well deserve the extra job title/pay/status (yes, I know, rest assured I did have my tongue firmly in my cheek there!) because nobody, but nobody, can clean the toilets/wash up/sort the toy cupboard

better than they can! And then they wonder why

nobody else ever cleans the toilets/washes up/sorts the toy cupboard and why they are always left behind at the end of a session…

It's important to remember that being a leader is not the same as being an 'advanced practitioner' (although if you are an advanced practitioner you probably do need leadership skills – don't worry, it will all get clearer, honest!). Many people in our field find themselves in some sort of management/leadership capacity because they are really good at the job they were doing previously – working with the children. And it is the case that there's a lot of advantages to being in that position – because as a leader you will not only know about good practice but also understand what the practical issues are around putting that into place in your setting.

But there are also disadvantages – because many of us end up feeling like we are still practitioners *really*, it's just that we've got a bit of extra responsibility/admin./paperwork on top of that. And unfortunately that's not the case – in fact it's exactly the opposite. What we actually need to do is to see ourselves as leaders first, with admin. and practitioner coming lower down our priority list in whichever order fits your setting!

(Probably worth mentioning here by the way that it has been known for people to find themselves in a leadership/management capacity and then realise that actually it's not want they want to be doing, so they decide to continue working as a practitioner instead. That's no bad thing in my book – sorry, no pun intended! - if it means that that person is more content in their work and the new leader is able to take on the role wholeheartedly.)

And whilst we're on the topic of working with the children, we just need a quiet word here about ratios. Now let me say straight away that there are lots of small settings who simply cannot, for reasons ranging from practical to financial, have a leader who is not counted in the ratios. No adventure playground manager worth their salt would sit in their office (if they have one!) for the whole time whilst a session is running, and although there are some room leaders in larger nurseries who are not counted in ratios, I think we would all agree that this is currently a luxurious exception!

But having said that, generally-speaking, if you work in a leadership capacity you need as much time off-ratio as possible - and I hope that by the end of this book it will be pretty clear why that is the case! Those of you who really do need to be counted in ratios need to work out how you will fulfil your leadership responsibilities alongside the hands-on time (and for many, the paperwork as well) – hopefully you will have some thoughts on that by the end of this book too.

Having said that, I've worked with many pre-school playgroups, with tiny numbers of staff and even tinier budgets, who have re-organised how things are done in their setting to free up some non-contact time for their leader. You see, it really all boils down to a question of priorities - knowing what your priorities as a leader are, making sure that you have the resources to put those priorities into place, and then doing your job according to those priorities. And in order to know what those priorities are, you really do have to understand what your role as a leader is all about first, so here goes....

Being in charge – in whatever shape or form that takes in your case – means that you are a leader, and therefore leadership is part of your role. Leadership is about providing direction, about setting out where it is you want people to go, and then helping them to get there – and/or taking action when it's pretty obvious that you're not (getting there, that is!). Leadership is about being the person who makes sure that everybody is working towards providing a really fantastic setting for children and ensuring that everybody in the setting is maintaining that focus. Leadership is therefore (uncomfortable as it may be for some) also about being the person who has to do something about it when people can't – or won't – fulfil that role.

At this point it's worth stressing that leadership **is** about the children that we work with. Ok, so many of you may feel like you will never see a child again when you go up the ranks (that doesn't have to be the case by the way but we'll come back to that later), but a leadership role, even when you are not counted in ratios, should be as much about the needs of children in your setting as having a 'hands-on' role. Somebody needs to have their eye on the bigger picture, to be able to step away from the day-to-day 'doing' and have a clear idea about the overall needs of the children in your setting and how you are all going to work to meet those changing needs on a long-term basis.

If everybody is focussed on the details of daily practice, there is a real danger that the bigger picture gets lost and so practice slips and slides or is not kept current and up-to-date. Leaders are the people who make sure that this doesn't happen, by keeping their focus on the bigger picture and making sure that the rest of the team know what that means for their day-to-day practice.

It is one of life's ironies of course that in many setting there are currently lots of leaders who are doing the exact opposite – instead of the 'bigger picture' stuff, they find themselves bogged down with minute details of running the setting – how many toilet rolls to buy, replacing the hoover bag, tidying that toy cupboard (again). This is not to say of course that these things are not important, but it is true to say that they are not part and parcel of leadership!

So leadership is actually about the children in your setting – not the adults. Which brings us onto another quite interesting – and vitally important – point. Because if leadership is about the children and not the adults, then it is also *definitely* not about keeping those adults - your staff team - happy.

Now I wouldn't be surprised if that comes as a bit of a shock to some of you, because at this point on our training courses there's usually several sharp intakes of breath! So you might want to pause, go back and read that last paragraph again and just take a minute to think about what that actually means…

…because for those of you who were surprised, it is a fundamentally different understanding of your role as a leader – and when we think about it logically, we can see why. Because 'keeping everybody happy' not only means that the focus gets taken away from the children, it's also a physical impossibility! Your setting – however small it might be - will be a mixture of individuals, with individual personalities, motivations, moods, wants and needs, all of which will change according to the day of the week, what side of bed people got up from that morning, their personal relationships… And to put it in a nutshell, if you put your energy into trying to meet all of those, not only will you lose sight of what the children need, but so will they!

That old saying is true you know – you really can't please all of the people all of the time - and in our line of work I hope you can see now why we shouldn't even start to try!

(I do realise that some of you will be thinking at this stage that it's all very well saying that we shouldn't try to keep people happy, but if they are not happy they will leave, and then what do we do? We all know about recruitment problems etc…but I think we need to start thinking not about personal happiness ('That's great, she's let me off the clearing up again because I had a bit of a strop about doing it last time') but professional happiness instead ('Clearing up isn't my favourite thing to do but I can see why it's important for the children to have lunch cleared away quickly so they don't hang around for ages getting bored and frustrated'). As leaders we need not to make friends, but to influence people – for the benefit of the children we work with.

So leadership is about setting a professional standard and having professional expectations of the professionals we work with. It's not about making sure everybody is happy – it's not even about making sure that everybody is 'friends' and/or likes each other – or even you!

YES, AND MY QUESTION IS — DO YOU THINK WE CAN BE FRIENDS?

We don't have to all be friends in our setting in order to deliver really great services to children — and in fact you could argue that in many cases it's better that we're not! Instead of trying to make everybody like us, we need to be clear on what it is we're trying to achieve for the children in our setting and how we are going to make sure that everybody gets there.

Now of course that's all very well saying that — sounds simple, doesn't it — as leaders we need to know where we're going and then make sure that everybody gets there. But it's the 'making sure' thing that's the tricky bit — because the key to all of this is people. It's common to hear people talking about 'leading a setting' — but it's easy to forget that that setting is made up of people — yes, all those individuals with different wants, needs, motivations we talked about earlier…And that, of course, is where the fun really starts!

So leadership is much more than just being in charge. It's not about doing it yourself, getting the paperwork done or even pleading and bargaining with your team to get things done! Neither is it about bossing people about or terrifying your team into submission. Leadership in our field is about defining, setting and making sure that everybody —

including you! – sticks to professional boundaries. It is about supporting and keeping everybody on track and knowing what to do when those professional boundaries are not achieved.

And for all of that to happen, as a leader you have to be pro-active, not reactive (or in other words, leading not following!) – so please, lead the way to Chapter 2!

Chapter 2
Mission – impossible?

So now we know who you are and what you're there for, let's now take a look at what it is that you are leading, and why you are leading it and where you are leading it to!

The assumption we'll start from is that you are, as we said in Chapter 1, in some sort of position of responsibility in some sort of setting. That setting could be an out-of-school club, nursery, family centre, playscheme, playbus or the dozens of other types of settings that look after children, support their play and/or learning.

So now I'd like you just to think about your 'type' of setting for the moment. Depending on what it is, there are thousands/hundreds/lots (pick your own multiple of 10!) of them across the UK. And whilst it's true to say that you can generally recognise the difference between a playscheme and a nursery (because they look like either a playscheme or a nursery!), it's also true to say that you can also recognise the difference between playschemes and between nurseries.

In other words, each setting within its type is pretty much unique. And that's not just because we use different buildings, buy equipment from different places, have different adults working there...Our settings are fundamentally different because of the very nature of the work we do. Because whatever our 'type' of setting, in general terms we are there to meet the needs of the children (for whatever particular purpose that may be – learning, childcare, community development, play etc), and the children in our settings will be unique. This means that our settings will be unique – because although we are all working to one set of professional guidance, legalisation etc, we will put this professional practice into place within the context of the needs of the children that we work with.

So your setting will be different from the out-of-school club/nursery/family centre down the road, it will be different from the out-of-school club/nursery/family centre on the other side of town, and it will be different from the other out-of-school clubs/nurseries/family centres that you get together with at meetings and conferences. Maybe sharing some of the same underpinning ethos, maybe having some common practice around day-to-day running, but because you are using this to support the children you work with, definitely different.

It's important that you know what it is that is unique about your setting, what it is that your setting offers *exactly* - because in a nutshell, that is what you are leading! So if you're happy enough with that as a concept, just park that thought for a minute and we'll come back to it…we just need to do the fun bit first!

Now this is where it starts to get interesting… trust me, it does! Because here we have you, the leader – and from Chapter 1 we know that your job is to make sure that your setting is achieving what it needs to achieve for the children who go there. And we've just been thinking about your setting, and how it will be unique in meeting the needs of those children.

But what is it exactly that your setting is trying to achieve? You, the leader (and the rest of your team, but we'll get to that later) need to know *exactly* what it is you are aiming for – because (and probably to bowdlerise some old Chinese saying), if you don't know where you are going, you are never going to know

which direction you are heading in or when you've got there. (Actually now I come to think of it it's probably a pop song from the '60's, but you get my drift...) And if you don't know any of those things, you start running round like a headless chicken –

and then we get back to that sorry state we were in in Chapter 1, and we don't want to go there again, do we?! (And yes, you got me – that last bit was just an excuse for a really silly cartoon - sorry, couldn't resist!)

What you need then, is something that tells you –

and everybody else — exactly what it is that your setting is about and, most importantly, what it aims to achieve for the children who go there. Because if you (all) know where you're heading, it is much easier for you, the leader, to lead people in that direction. Now believe me, I'm no great fan of management jargon, but we do need to use some

NOW THEN, I NEED A NICE, CONFUSING
WAY OF SAYING "LOOKING AFTER CHILDREN"

now, because what we're actually talking about here is a mission statement. A mission statement is a simple sentence (yes, usually just the one) which describes what it is that an organisation needs to achieve. (And if the jargon really does put you off, think 'aim of the setting' instead – it does the same job, but you see if I'd called this chapter 'aim of the setting' it would have completely ruined the cartoons!)

Just a word here to those of you who are doing your leading for parts of your settings – room leaders in nurseries or heads of distinct services in children's centres, for example. It may well be that the larger organisation in which you work will have a mission statement which encompasses all of the work that the setting does, but having a 'mini mission statement' for your own discrete area of work can be really helpful in getting your team focussed on what it is that your part of the whole setting does. So although we're going to talk about setting mission statements for the rest of this chapter, use the same ideas to develop your own mission statement – they really do work!

So your mission — should you choose to accept it — is to write down on that nice blank page opposite exactly what it is that your setting should be achieving for children — or in other words, write down your mission statement / aim of your setting. This might take a few minutes so feel free to make a cup of tea whilst you're thinking about it....

Ok, are you back with me now? If you are, my guess is that one of several things has just happened...

Often when people do this exercise their brains do a back-flip, or they simply freeze. The old panic sets in and, if this has just happened to you, apart from a few random words or doodlings of the cat, you've probably pretty much got a blank page staring back at you.

Some people say 'Oh yes, we've got that in our operational plan,' and then stare blankly into space for ages and ages, desperately trying to remember what it is. If this is you — you're not alone, so don't worry about it, we'll get there by the end of the chapter!

Sometimes people say 'Oh yes, we've got that in our operational plan,' and can dash it off word for word and then feel pretty smug about it. If this is you — congratulations! And if the next section doesn't ring any bells with you because it doesn't apply to you, then double congratulations and have another cup of tea to celebrate while the rest of us just grapple with the next bit...

Because what happens to most people is they write something that goes a bit like this....

"Happy Days nursery/playscheme/unique childcare setting offers safe, happy, friendly, stimulating, high-quality childcare in a secure, child-centred environment."

Now if that looks anything like what you've written, or if you didn't write anything but think that sounds like a pretty good idea of what you should have written, please read on, because I'm afraid you don't get your second cup of tea yet... You see, there's rather a lot of work we need to do now, because – well, frankly, and I do hope I'm not going to shock you here, but there's just so many things wrong with that as a mission statement it's pretty hard to know where to start!

First of all, remember what we said about your setting being unique? Well, the first problem we've got is the bit about most people coming up with something along those lines – because if the majority of settings have mission statements like that, how unique does that make your setting?!

How much justice does that do to the individual work you are doing with the children, how does that describe how your nursery/playscheme/unique childcare setting specifically meets the specific needs of the specific children in your specific setting? (I know there's too many 'specifics' in that sentence by the way, but there's a specific reason for that which we'll get to in a minute…) The answer is that it doesn't – all it tells the world is that "our nursery/playscheme/unique childcare setting is just like the one down the road"….not totally inspiring really, is it?

And that brings us to our second problem, which in terms of you leading your staff team is probably even more significant. I don't want to go all management-speak on you, but a mission statement/aim of the setting should inspire people, and in particular it should inspire your team. Every member of staff should know not only why they come to work but also why they come to work at your setting - and also be able to communicate

that to anybody and everybody else. We're drifting into Chapter 4 territory so we'll leave that there, but for now just hang on to the fact that your team need to feel motivated, and as something that could help you to motivate them I'm afraid this mission statement just doesn't do it!

And thirdly (yes, sorry, there's more!), as a leader you need to have a clear direction in which to lead your team. Remember, if you don't know where you're going etc… The trouble with having the 'safe, happy, friendy, secure' variety of mission statement is that I defy anybody to tell me – specifically – what that actually means, and if you can't actually say what it means, it's going to be pretty impossible to lead anybody anywhere with it!

And the reason that we can't lead anybody anywhere with those words is that they are all too vague and woolly… 'Safe', for example, is a relative concept, and anyway, do we really want children to be 'safe'? Safe enough, definitely, appropriately safe, maybe – but safety, meaning the absence of any type of hazard, is not a desirable state for children to be in. (Please see The Buskers Guide to Risk for more on this topic and then I can save us all a rant here!) 'Happy' is a nice word, but are we really saying that we want children to be happy all the time? Because that would be a fib – we know that experiencing and developing a range of emotions is good for children – and a permanent state of happiness would actually be psychologically rather dangerous!

The other difficulty we've got with these words, apart from the fact that we don't actually mean them, is that they can all be interpreted in lots of different ways – and more to the point, they can be interpreted (and mis-interpreted!) in lots of different ways by your team. And take it from me, this is not a desirable state of affairs to be in…because as we saw in Chapter 1, the role of the leader is to get everybody working in the same direction to achieve the aim of the setting. This simply can't be done if everybody is working to

their own idea of what 'safe, happy, friendly, secure' actually means, because everybody will be applying their own understanding of those words to the children they are working with and the setting as a whole.

And if then, as the leader, you need to talk to someone about how you need them to do something differently, you open up a whole can of worms…but that's a particular joy we'll leave to think about later on….

Now at this point some of you might be thinking – yes, ok, see your point in theory, but really it's common sense, isn't it? Surely everybody knows what we mean by 'stimulating' – we don't really mean that the kids have to be 'up and at 'em' every minute we're with them, we have a balanced routine, everybody knows that….

Well yes, and I can see your point too if that's any help, but that still leaves us a couple of things to think about. First of all, you can't really assume that everybody does have the same sort of ideas and understanding. Your team will come from a range of different backgrounds and experiences and whatever their level of professional practice, they will have been influenced by many things in both their personal and professional lives. So 'common sense' doesn't really help us in this instance, because it depends on whose version of 'common sense' we are going to go by!

BUT YOU SAID TO DO THE DISHES
WHILE YOU WERE OUT.

And secondly, if we really do know what we mean, why don't we just say it? That way we don't leave room for various interpretations that might turn out to be more trouble than they're worth in the long-run. It always seems to me that our field has a collective gift, one that is a great tradition but is not, unfortunately, entirely useful. It's the gift of word-salad – we use words and terms which are entirely weird and wonderful, we even make them up sometimes, and then we moan about the fact that our team/parents/our headteacher/the rest of the universe doesn't understand us. Take a look at these words and try to really think about what they mean…

❖ child-centred
❖ high quality
❖ age-appropriate
❖ partnership with parents
❖ inclusion

Can you see where I'm coming from on this one? We can be 'child-centred' until that particular child wants chocolate spread sandwiches for her tea every night – and then we're going to stop being 'child-centred' because that's not good for them. We can do 'partnership with parents' until his parent doesn't want him dressing up in girls' clothes – and then we're not in partnership anymore, we're going to have a quiet chat instead to inform them of the error of their ways…

Of course, there's a good old debate to be had here – I know there will be some of you now yelling at this page, 'But that's not what partnership with parents is *supposed* to mean.' But this is a Buskers Guide and, Big though it maybe, we still haven't got the space, sorry – and anyway, that's sort of the point. Because the more vague and woolly the terminology is that we use, the more meanings you can get out of that terminology, and as a field we excel in shifting those meanings until they're not quite what they are *supposed* to be. You for example might be crystal clear on the 'correct' definition of inclusion, but I've worked with settings where, in the name of 'inclusion', nobody can play football because Fred uses a wheelchair to get about and can't run.

Anyway, where were we? Ah yes, I was trying to convince you to say what you mean and mean what you say...Those woolly words won't help you to lead your team I'm afraid as they allow just too much room for manoeuvre, so as a leader you need to be crystal clear in your own mind about what it is you want your team to achieve for the children in your setting.

So, now's your chance – are you ready for another blank page?!

Use this one to make some notes about exactly what it is you need your setting to achieve – and as a bit of a tip, make sure you avoid all those confusing words on page 33.

Now my guess is that many of you found that quite hard – those woolly words really do seem to get inside our heads don't they?! And the trouble is that when they get taken away we get a bit stuck. But don't panic, it will come eventually – instead of trying to replace those words, just try to focus instead on your setting and the children who are in it. What do you want for them, what can your setting help them to achieve, what should your setting offer to the children who go there? Are there particular milestones you are helping them to reach, do you want their time in your setting to give them particular skills, be that social, emotional or educational skills, can you describe how the children should benefit from being at your setting in terms of their overall development, and/or why it's so important that they have access to the type of experiences you are offering?

There is also another way to look at creating a mission statement, and that is by using existing frameworks which have already set out what it is your setting should achieve for children. At the time of writing, frameworks such as the Playwork Principles, the Early Years Foundation Stage, local and national quality assurance schemes, inspection frameworks and so on all set standards of how settings can best meet the needs of the children they are working with. So does your setting want achieve an 'excellent' at inspection, to meet the Early Years Foundation Stage for all children, be able to demonstrate the Playwork Principles in practice at all times, consistently achieve the local authority kitemark for childcare settings in your area…?

Remember that your mission statement needs to be about your setting, so think carefully about what is most important for your setting and for the children you work with. Sure, it's great to always get brilliant inspection reports – but maybe there's something else that could make a bigger difference to the children you work with if you focussed your team in that direction instead. There isn't a right or wrong answer to developing a mission statement – and unlike 'safe, happy, friendly, secure', it is certainly not a case of one size fits all, because as we said earlier, your setting is unique. So take another look at your notes on page 35 and see if you can come up with a sentence which truly describes what your setting is about.

And once you've got

GO ON, YOU CAN DO IT. THINK OF IT MORE AS MISSION-A-BIT-TRICKY.

something down that you think starts to describe your setting (and nobody else's!), there is an acronym that you can apply to your statement to see whether you have really got rid of those vague and woolly words! Your mission statement needs to be SMART, which stands for specific (yep, there's that word again!), measurable, achievable, realistic and timed (although we won't worry about the timed bit with your mission statement as we will assume that your setting is going to be there forever!).

Specific means that your mission statement needs to be extremely clear and precise in the language that it uses. Can any of the words or phrases be (mis) interpreted – have any of *those* words (you know the ones!) crept in by mistake? *Measurable* means that you need to be able to see whether you are doing it/have done it or not, because if you can't measure it then you can't achieve it so your mission statement won't be *achievable* – remember that Chinese proverb/1960's pop song about you won't know if you've got there if you don't know where you're going? And if it's not *realistic*, then you won't be able to achieve it anyway, so you have to be sure that when you set your mission statement that it is something that your setting can realistically expect to achieve.

By applying SMART to your mission statement and seeing if it stands up to the test, you can see whether it will be useful to you as a leader in setting out the direction for the rest of your team. But make sure that you are patient with yourself – you won't get it right first time, and over a period of time your thinking about your mission statement will develop and so you will need to review it on a regular basis. The important thing is that you have a clear mission statement that your whole team can work towards – with your support.

Now there will of course be those of you who have just gone through the entire chapter and have come out the other end thinking – well that's all very well, but I work in a chain of settings and we all share the same mission statement…So your mission – should you choose to accept it - is to do one of two things. You can either see if that mission statement is SMART and therefore useful to you in leading your team – and if it isn't, then try to make it more useful! Or if that's really not possible, how about developing your own, perhaps 'unofficial' mission statement just for your team?

So far so good – end of Chapter 2 and we've already got a leader with a clear role and a setting with a clear purpose. When it comes to being able to lead a setting those are the two things which are the most important to be clear on – and then after that everything else just sort of falls into place. Trust me – onwards and upwards to Chapter 3!

MISSION ACCOMPLISHED

Chapter 3
A mission shared...

Now we've got our mission statement sorted (or as sorted as it's going to be for now!) and we're clear about what it is we're trying to achieve in our setting, we need to think about how we're going to get that mission across in our settings. Because this mission statement that you've just poured your heart and soul into in the last chapter needs to be part of your every day practice, and it also needs to be part of the everyday practice of your team. It's not like a policy that sits on the top shelf in a nice file, gathering dust (ahem!) – it should be the foundation of everything you do in your setting (and no, that doesn't mean you get to bury it either!). And if your team can't get up in the morning and chant your mission statement before their feet hit the floor, you should want to know the reason why!

So in this chapter we're going to think about some of the ways that you can incorporate your mission statement into different parts of the setting, so that everybody knows what your setting is doing for the benefit of the children you work with.

And just a word of warning before we set off – this chapter will probably feel quite short, but don't let that catch you out, I'm afraid this bit often involves a lot of work – sorry!

The obvious place to start is the **setting brochure** / information leaflet / parents pack or whatever that type of thing is called in your setting! Most settings have booklets or pieces of paper of some description that give parents general information about the setting and how it works. If you start this off with your all-singing, all-dancing mission statement you can then go on to explain exactly what this means for their children.

For example, if part of your mission statement is about supporting children to develop independence skills, then you will need to explain what this means in your setting and that sometimes it might result in Johnny goes home with the odd scrape!

Now some of you might at this point be thinking – yes but hang on, parents like to hear words like 'happy, friendly, safe' etc – and why should we blind them with science if that's what they want to hear? But remember that we said earlier that your setting is unique and it needs to reflect that in its mission statement. It's also much fairer to parents if they know what their signing up to, and then maybe you won't get so many complaints when Johnny does go home with a minor injury! And there's another really crucial reason that we need to communicate what it is that we are offering children. We need to be clear that we have professional values and intentions for the children that we work with – 'safe, happy, friendly' etc just makes us sound like glorified babysitters!

YES, OUR AIM IS TO OFFER SAFE, HAPPY, FRIENDLY, STIMULATING CHILDCARE...

And whilst we're on the subject of parents understanding what we do, let's just take a moment to think about **conversations** we have with parents. Do we refer to our mission statement when we are describing what their children are / have been doing in our setting, or do we use the language and important bits of our mission statement to help parents to understand how it all fits together? For those settings which have 'handover' conversations with parents at the end of each session, do we make sure that we take the opportunity to get the message across about how we've put our mission statement into practice today – or do we just say something quite vague like, 'Johnny's had a good day, he played in the sand and by the way, could you sign the accident book while you're here?'

Now of course some of you may be wondering why we're talking about parents, when so far up until now we have been talking about leadership in terms of your professional team. But it's important that your parents are as clear as your team about your mission statement, so that your team are able to have those types of professional discussions with parents and it won't take them by surprise or be the first time that they've heard that that's what you actually do with their children! And of course it works the other way round too – encouraging your team to talk to parents about their children in terms of your mission statement means that individual team members also become clearer and more confident not only about the mission statement itself, but also their role in achieving that mission statement for the children they work with.

Which, of course, as a leader is what you need to achieve – making sure that all of your team members not only know what the mission statement is, but how it works in practice and what it means for their role. For existing members of staff this is most easily done through regular **supervision sessions** and **annual appraisal** systems, setting targets and priorities according to how individual job roles will contribute to achieving the mission statement. (Sorry we haven't got any more room to go into supervision and appraisal here, but it will be the subject of a future Big Buskers if that's any help!)

There are of course lots of other opportunities for helping members of your team to understand what the mission statement means in practice. Some settings for example will have **end of day** *evaluations* – and if this is the case in your setting, does this mean that the conversation is focussed on how you, for example, supported children's emotional development, or did you just all breath a sigh of relief that nobody got killed, made a note to buy more clay for tomorrow and then all went home? And then of course there are the **team meetings**...In my experience really worthwhile team meetings focus on how we are achieving / what's getting in the way of us achieving what we need to do for the children in our setting (as set out in the you-know-what!), rather than the ones that end up in endless boring debates about...

....sorry, just the very thought made me drift off there! Where were we?!

Oh yes, good leaders make the most of all the opportunities they can to focus their teams' minds on what they are there for – or in other words, to lead them in the direction they need them to go. And of course there are lots of opportunities to do this with new members of staff – even before new jobs are advertised, **job descriptions** can be reviewed to see whether they reflect what the setting is actually about (or whether they are just a lot of words on a page that could describe any job in any setting). And during **induction periods** new members of the team need to be introduced to the mission statement in terms of what that means in their role and in their day-to-day work.

New members of staff will of course be introduced to your **policies** (once the dust has been blown of them, of course!) and it's important that your policies also reflect your mission statement. Like job descriptions, policies can end up as a load of almost meaningless words on a page, whereas actually they can be really useful pieces of paper which explain to both your team (new and old) and anybody else who needs to know (parents, funders, inspectors etc) exactly how you put your mission statement into practice. What for example does 'supporting independence skills' mean in terms of health and safety – and does our health and safety policy tell us that, because if it doesn't, it should!

And finally, there is another really invaluable way of getting your mission statement across to the rest of your team, and that is by role-modelling. Remember we said in Chapter 1 that those of you who have to be counted in ratios can use that 'hands on' time as part of your leadership role? Well, this is one of the ways that it works beautifully – because whilst you are working with the children you can be role-modelling parts of your mission statement for the rest of the team. Perhaps you will be standing back and observing, for example, when children are trying out new things for themselves, or perhaps you will be offering choices to children instead of insisting that they stick to the normal routine even when they are deeply absorbed in something. Those types of practice can then be discussed at your team meeting as examples of how you would like your team to encourage children's independence skills (or whatever it is that you want them to do in line with your mission statement).

So a mission shared is not a mission halved - as we can see from this chapter, it's actually exactly the opposite! If used in the right way, it should be a mission which grows and spreads, and as it grows and spreads it should influence good practice and build a shared understanding of why your setting exists.

But of course, all this doesn't just happen –

remember that we said at the end of Chapter 1 that leadership is proactive and not reactive? So the next chapter is going to be about the personal skills that you as a leader need to be able to show the way...

Chapter 4
The art of persuasion...

So now we know that our leadership role is about being out in front, the person who is setting out the vision for what the setting will achieve for children, and we've looked at lots of different ways of communicating that vision to your team. But we can't leave it there I'm afraid – because of those individuals we talked about in Chapter 1. It would be really nice, wouldn't it, to think that, once we've done all that hard work in describing what the vision is and getting it out there, that our teams all stand back in amazement and congratulate us – and then just proceed to get on with it, perfectly and without question.

But of course this is incredibly rare occurrence (so if it happens like that in your setting, please do let me know!), because good leadership in any team means change. Yes it may be the case that you'll make some changes in your setting as a result of reading this book, but it's also true that good leaders are always looking to develop things, to move things on, for all those reasons that we talked about in Chapter 1 about meeting the needs of the children we work with. Leadership is not about maintaining the status quo, it's about keeping your eye firmly on that bigger picture and taking your team to where that bigger picture tells you you need to go, in the best interests of the children you work with.

And whilst of course it's not good for teams to be in a constant state of change just for the sake of it, let's face it, in our field things change all the time! Not only do we have to think about the changing needs of the children in our settings, but we've also got changes happening all the time in the wider professional field – changes in legislation, changes in good practice, changes in inspection regimes… Change happens to us, as well as being initiated by us, and as professionals we need to not only keep up with changes but also be proactive in putting them into place for the benefit of the children we work with.

But that is then where the fun starts…because there are quite a lot of us human beings of the adult variety who are not very good at change of any sort. So be it small changes (how to better organise that toy cupboard) or large ones (new ways of working needed by changes in legislation), you could be in line for a variety of not-so-positive responses from your team that sound something like this;

- ❖ it's not been done like that before
- ❖ it's change and therefore it isn't good
- ❖ it was tried before but it didn't work, so no point in trying it again
- ❖ it wasn't my idea so it must be bad
- ❖ no time/energy/resources so might as well stay as we are

…and so on!

Now as a leader it's important to see these responses – and any like them! – not as a dead end, or even as a negative thing – because we're now getting down to the real nitty-gritty of what leadership is about! Remember that all through this book so far we've talked about taking people with us, showing the way, being pro-active not reactive…well, now finally here's our chance! Because the key word here is *influence*. To be able to do all of those things, and to be a good leader, we have to be able to have an effect on the behaviour of others – and in the case of our working with children, to influence the professional practice of others.

And in order to do this we need some vital personal and professional skills; time management, delegation, confidence, assertiveness, reflective practice, and creativity.

Time management might not sound like an obvious skill required for influencing people, but influencing people does take time – and working with somebody to develop their practice does take more time than doing whatever it is that needs doing yourself! It's all too easy (especially in our field it seems to me) for leaders to say 'Oh it's quicker to do it myself!', but then end up wondering why they get so exhausted/stressed or just down right fed up so quickly or so often!

I JUST DON'T KNOW
WHERE THE TIME GOES...

This of course is where **delegation** is such an important skill to develop – knowing to whom you can pass work onto and when it is appropriate to do this. Delegation is only appropriate when members of your team have the necessary support and/or skills to take on new tasks or roles – it's not a good idea to give other people some of your workload just because you haven't got the time to do stuff! Some of the key questions you need to ask before delegating work include;

❖ has this person demonstrated any skills which would help them in this task?
❖ what sort of training/support do they need to be able to take on this task?
❖ how much time do I need to spend with them to enable them to take on this task?
❖ how will I know when they are ready to take on this task without close supervision?

All of which, I'm sure you will have gathered by now, will take time – time to work out how you get somebody up to speed with a new role, and time to put in that support that they need to get to grips with it. Which of course, brings us back to time management…

The key to time management is understanding what the priorities are, both in the short-term and the long-term – and the long-term priority for you as a leader has to be to get your team to deliver really good practice in your setting. And whilst it's really easy to believe that you don't have time to do supervisions/appraisals/training courses for your own professional development/team meetings/observations on sessions etc, these are all really important tools for helping you to do just that. In fact in my experience what stops leaders having time to do those things is that they are too busy 'fire-fighting', or in other words being reactive rather than proactive. Because by dealing with stuff as it comes up, instead of taking the time to put systems into place that might stop those awkward situations happening in the first place, we get ourselves into a bit of a self-fulfilling prophecy – because the things that stop us from having time are the very things that would make us time if only we took the time to put them in place in the first place!

One situation that often gets mentioned as a time thief in our field is having to be in ratios because of staff sickness, holidays etc. But as leaders we have to make a decision about priorities here – yes, of course we might need to step in in an emergency, but being reactive like this is not a good long-term strategy, because it will eat up lots of time that we could be spending doing other things. So our priority should be to think about how we avoid this happening in the future and invest some time to develop other ways of dealing with this type of inevitable occurrence – because actually, although I used the word 'emergency' earlier, we know that it's not such an unusual thing for staff to be off and/or be off unexpectedly. Being pro-active rather than re-active often means spending time now to avoid spending more time in the future – and another fundamental law of time management is that what looks like an emergency often isn't!

So as leaders it's important that we do that stepping back thing as we talked about in Chapter 1 – to look at that bigger picture as summed up by our mission statement and to work out what our priorities are according to that, rather than always reacting to what's in front of us.

But of course in order to be able to set and work to your own priorities and those of the setting, rather than whatever anybody else thinks is most important at the time, you have to have **confidence** – confidence in yourself and in your decision-making abilities. (It's important to bear in mind that this is a different type of confidence from the confidence that practitioners need, and many people in leadership roles in our field have huge amounts of confidence when it comes to working with children but then seem to lose it almost entirely when it comes to influencing adults!)

Now the reason that confidence is so important when it comes to leadership is that, oddly enough, people who exude confidence are seen as more competent than those who don't. And bearing in mind what we said earlier about many people not being so comfortable with change, if you have to change the way you are behaving/working, which are you going to feel more comfortable with – the leader who looks like she's going to see it through and it will all be alright in the end, or the leader who hesitates, appears not to be so sure, or even cajoles?!

So if you want to persuade people that change is a good thing, that they really do need to follow your lead, then buckets of confidence needs to be the order of the day I'm afraid – whether you feel it or not!

Which brings us nicely onto **assertiveness** skills – because confident people are assertive. Now it's important to remember that assertiveness is not like an umbrella that you put up or down depending on whether it's raining or not – it's not a case of 'being assertive' when the going gets rough and then going back to 'normal' when the stormy weather has passed.

I WONDER IF YOU'D MIND AWFULLY
IF I HAD A GO AT BEING ASSERTIVE NOW?

Assertiveness should be a state of being, a permanent state of mind – not to be confused with aggressiveness, assertive behaviour is simply behaviour which takes as its starting point that you have a right to ask for what you need. Or to put that in a professional context - as the leader you have the right to ask other people in your team to achieve whatever it is they need to achieve for the children in your setting (and, by the way, you have to have the confidence in your own judgement to feel that whatever that it is right).

Now, if they are doing it right, it's actually easier to tell when leaders are not being assertive than when they are! Because when they don't feel that it's ok for them to influence the practice of others, they start saying some very peculiar things that sound a bit like this;

- ❖ Do you think you could…
- ❖ Would it be a good idea if we…
- ❖ I wonder if we should..
- ❖ Could we possibly…
- ❖ Would you mind just…

…and I have to confess my all-time favourite;

- ❖ Could you do me a favour and…

Now I would guess that there are some of you who are now wincing horribly – but hopefully at least you know why you are wincing horribly! As leaders, as the people in charge, responsible for delivering a really great service to the children in our setting, are we *really* asking people if they'd mind awfully doing their jobs in order to make that happen?!

I WONDER IF YOU'D MIND... ER, WELL, YOU KNOW... DOING YOUR JOB PLEASE?

And the other problem with that type of language is that people do tend to hear what they want to hear from it. Because 'Could you do me a favour and de-tox those tables?' could actually sound like there is — and always has been and therefore always will be — an option, that de-toxing tables before snack time is an 'extra', not something that is expected as part of somebody's daily job role (and is therefore hardly worth mentioning).

So we all need to try to keep the toy cupboard tidier.

One really useful rule of thumb is that when you are being assertive, pretty much all of your sentences will start with 'I'. So instead of some of the little delights (!) above, you will hear yourself saying things such as;

- ❖ 'I'd like you to…'
- ❖ 'I need you to…'
- ❖ 'I've noticed that…'
- ❖ 'I think it's important that…'

Now it has to be said here that many people find this way of talking uncomfortable, and therefore start saying things such as, 'But shouldn't you take other people's views/feelings into account?' Well yes, to some extent – but not if it's something fundamental like cleaning tables or emptying chemical toilets. Because provided that the right training has happened to enable them to know that this is part of their job role and needs doing on a regular basis, then there really isn't any debate to be had – it just needs to be done, not as a favour, to you or anybody else, including the children!

Just to also mention that sometimes it's easier to reject a different way of behaving by throwing out such objections because it feels so uncomfortable – think about the various possible negative reactions to change we looked at earlier! But assertive behaviour is first and foremost about taking responsibility – for what you think, feel and need, and for people who do not act assertively that can feel like a big change. The good news however that if we are clear about what we think, feel and need then there is less room for that (mis) interpretation on behalf of our teams and therefore more likelihood that we will succeed in leading our teams to where we all need to be as result!

Of course we will only be able to tell if we are being assertive, as opposed to non-assertive or aggressive, if we have developed our **reflective practice** so that it is a useful tool for us to use to think about the way that we are behaving when leading our teams. Reflective practice is often seen as a process of questioning about how something went, where as in actual fact it should be a learning tool for future development. So if you are trying to think about whether an interaction with a member of your team was assertive or not, you could use the following model to reflect on the interaction....

1. Intention – what was it that I set out to do?

    To be assertive – to clearly state what I need to happen without being aggressive or cajoling!

2. Experience – what actually happened?

   Well, we had a bit of a pleasant chat and then I tried to ask her to be on time for work but she ended up going off in a huff!

3. Action – what part did I play in what actually happened?

   I was being quite normal until we got to the bit about her being late and then I got a bit anxious about telling her to be on time and raised my voice and was a bit abrupt.

4. Outcome – what happened as a result of my actions?

   She got really wound up and went off in a huff. We didn't resolve the issue and I was left feeling really cross.

5. Development – what can I learn from this for the next time a similar situation occurs?

   I think I was aggressive rather than assertive, because I got anxious about talking to her about a difficult subject. Next time I need to stay calm and remember that it's ok for me to ask her to get to work on time – after all, it's part of her job!

We do have to be very aware of both ourselves and what's happening for this sort of reflective practice to be helpful and effective – and of course the other thing we need to be is completely honest with ourselves. After all, if we are leading our teams for the benefit of the children, then we are also part of that process – and our own practice won't develop if we are not willing to be honest – and even critical – about our own behaviour and practice.

Of course it's also important as a leader that we are encouraging our teams to be reflective practitioners, and this is then another opportunity for role-modelling in your setting!

The last skill which is essential for leaders in our field is *creativity*. Now this may sound a little odd, given some of the blood, sweat and tears we've had to put in so far (!), but the reason why creativity, and more specifically, creative thinking, are important is that we work with people. And as we said before, not only are people different, but we work in a field where very often there is no right or wrong. Apart from the obvious situations where 'right or wrong' definitely does apply, our work is more than often about trying things out, seeing how something works, or even indeed seeing *if* something works. Leaders, by the very nature of their job role, cannot be scared of change – because change in our field will happen anyway, and our job is to take others through that change.

So a leadership approach to change needs to sound something like;

- ❖ What if…
- ❖ I wonder how…
- ❖ What would happen if we did it that way?
- ❖ What have I learnt to help me….
- ❖ Does it have to be like that?

…and hopefully by role-modelling this approach your team will take on some of that curious and creative way of thinking too!

And finally...

Hopefully this first Big Buskers Guide has helped you to get a clear understanding of what being a leader in our field is about. It is about setting the agenda, having a vision, showing the way – and then taking others with you to ensure really great practice in your setting.

It is not about clearing up after people (either literally or metaphorically!), being the person who just does the paperwork, or the person who gets to deal with all the problems.

It is however about;

- ❖ Being clear on what your setting is there to achieve
- ❖ Communicating that vision to your team (and anybody else who needs to know)
- ❖ Using a range of skills to influence the practice of your team to achieve that vision
- ❖ Putting in place systems and structures to help you monitor that practice and work with others to improve it where necessary.

So now tell me you've got time to clean the toilets!

Further Reading

About Building your Self Confidence. (print on demand)
Bath: Scriptographic Publications Ltd.

Adair, J & Allen, M (2003) *Concise Time Management and Personal Development.* London: Thorogood.

Adair, J (2002) *100 Greatest Ideas for Effective Leadership and Time Management.*
Oxford: Capstone Publishing Ltd.

Ashman, C & Green, S (2004) *Self Development for Early Years Managers (Managing in the Early Years).*
London: David Fulton Publishers.

Dickenson, A (1982) *A Woman in Your Own Right: Assertiveness and You.* London: Quartet Books.

Fleming, I & Hailstone, P (2003 5th revised edition) *The Time Management Pocket Book.*
Alresford: Management Pocketbooks.

Gillen, T (1997) *Assertiveness.* London: Chartered Institute of Personnel & Development.

Heller, R (1998) *How to Delegate.*
London: Dorling Kindersley Ltd.

Hindle, T (1998) *Manage your Time.*
London: Dorling Kindersley Ltd.

Isles-Buck, E & Newstead, S (2003) *Essential Skills for Managers of Child-Centred Settings.* London: David Fulton Publishers.

Lewis, D (1995) *10-Minute Time and Stress Management.* London: Piatkus Books.

Lindenfield, G (1992) *Assert Yourself: A Self-help Assertiveness Programme for Men and Women.* London: Thorsons.

Maitland, I (1999) *Managing your Time.* London: Chartered Institute of Personnel & Development.

Michelli, D (1998 2nd Ed.) *Successful Assertiveness in a Week.* London: Hodder & Stoughton Ltd.

Righton, C (2006) *The Life Audit.* London: Hodder Mobius.

Woodhull, A V (1997) *The New Time Manager.* Abingdon: Gower Publishing Ltd.